D1609359

Did you know that newborn babies See mainly White and Black?

This book is perfect for babies because High contrast Images are easier for newborns and babies to interpret, Little babies Have an easier time focusing on high contrast objects during the stage of Visual development. and this book is specially designed for your little baby's eyes to explore. With simple Independence day-themed Images. to help support your Baby'svision development.

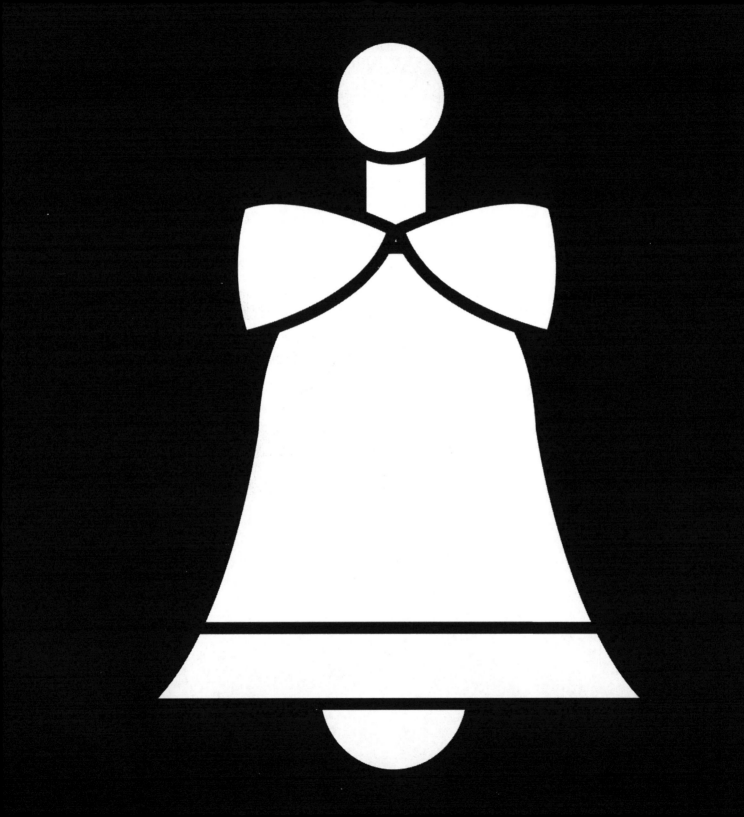

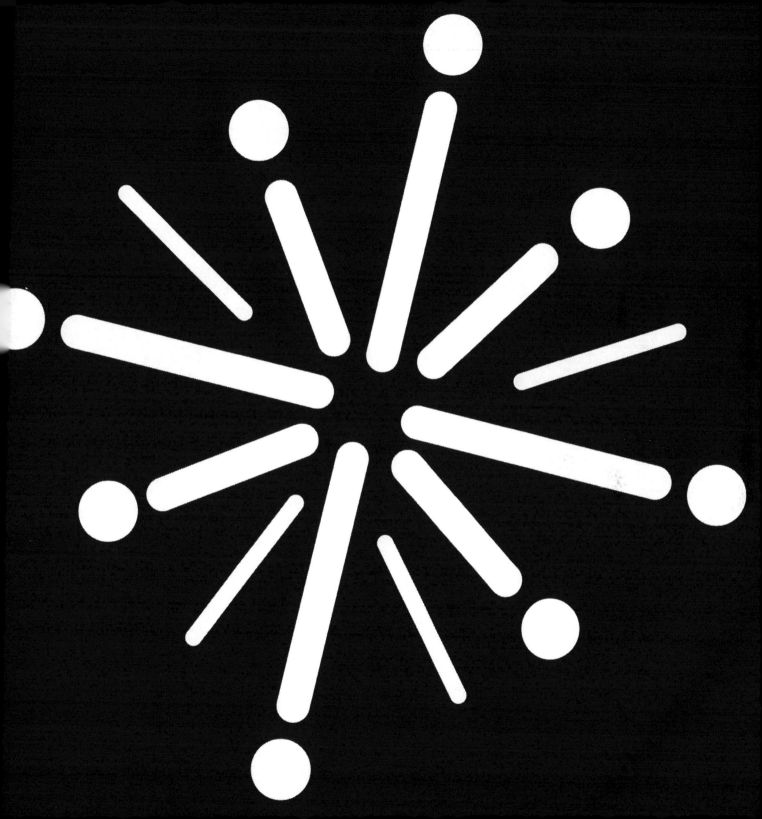

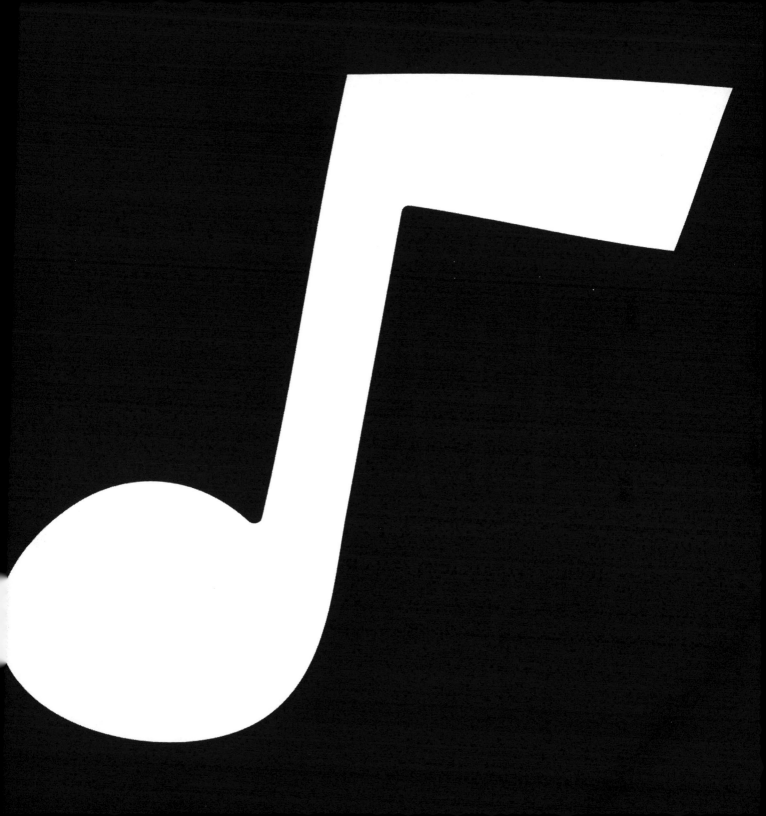

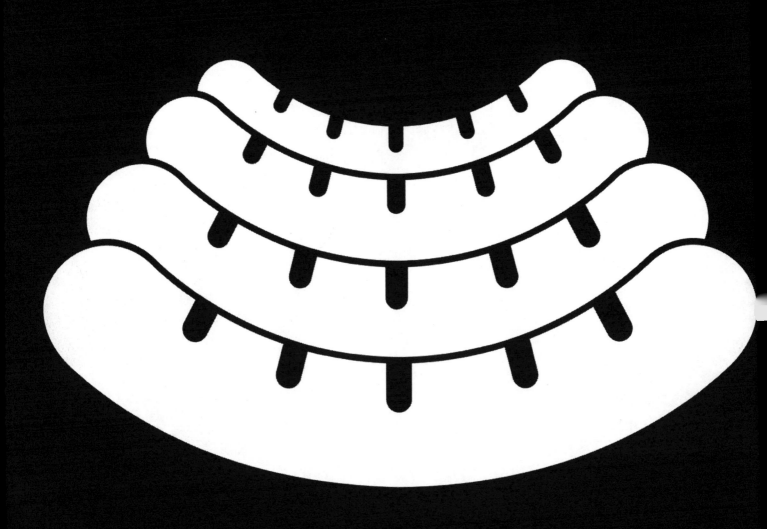

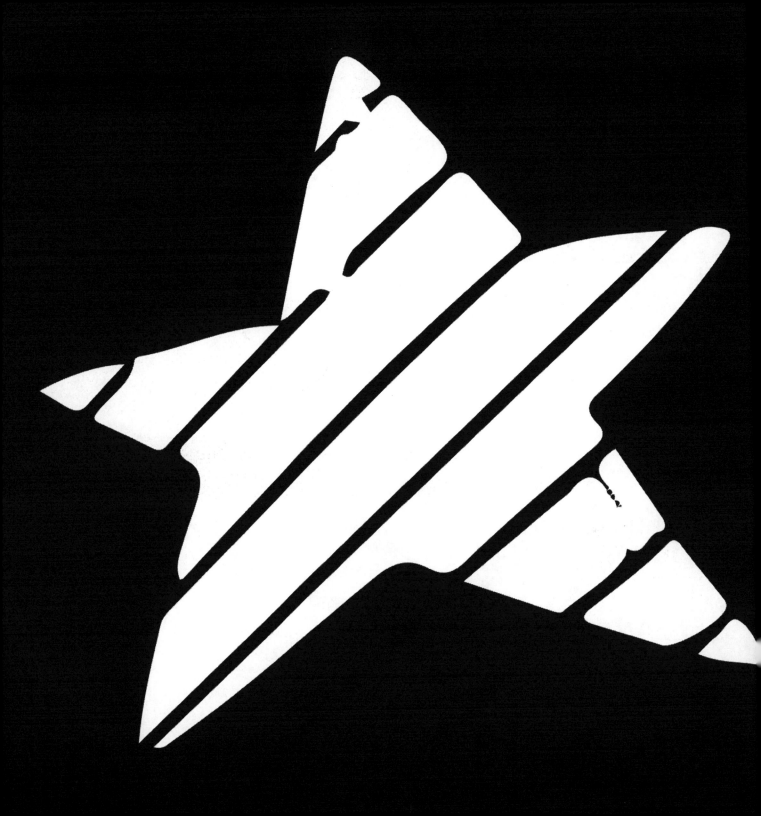

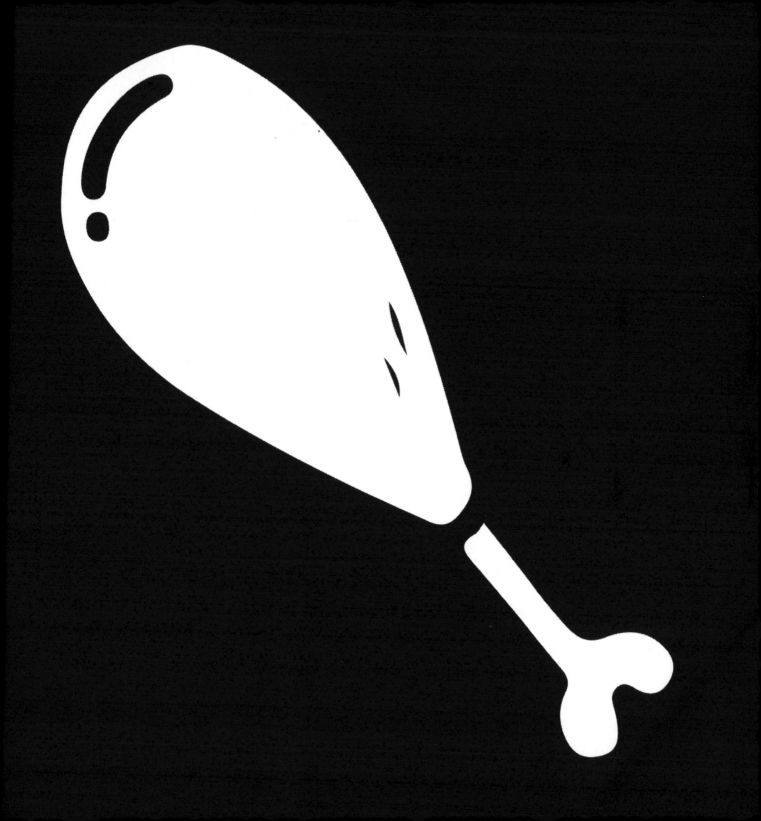

Made in the USA
Monee, IL
13 June 2022